IMAGES
of America

WASHINGTON
COUNTY

IMAGES
of America

WASHINGTON
COUNTY

Joseph P. Soares

ARCADIA
PUBLISHING

Published by Arcadia Publishing
Charleston, South Carolina

Library of Congress Catalog Card Number: 2005933100

For all general information contact Arcadia Publishing at:
Telephone 843-853-2070
Fax 843-853-0044
E-mail sales@arcadiapublishing.com
For customer service and orders:
Toll-Free 1-888-313-2665

Visit us on the Internet at www.arcadiapublishing.com

CONTENTS

ACKNOWLEDGMENTS

Walter Rogers must be acknowledged as one of the great photographers of his time. We in Washington County are lucky that Rogers exercised his talents here. Having lived in this area all my life, I sometimes tend to take for granted the rural beauty of this area. But when I look at photographs from the past and see how little the rural character has changed, I realize how lucky we are to reside in a place such as Washington County.

As the author, I am truly grateful to the local historians who took the time to help me with this project. I first have to thank Hope Greene Andrews for her interest and encouragement throughout this project. Her in-depth knowledge of our local history provided an invaluable contribution to this book. I would like to thank everyone at the Langworthy Public Library who helped in my search for information. The Gladys Segar and Gladys Palmer Collections were very useful. The generosity of this library will not be forgotten. I would also like to thank Richard Baton for his contribution to the book.

Much appreciation is extended to the following people and organizations that helped provide information for this project: Josephine Langworthy, Jane L. Smith, Gayle Waite, Hopkinton Historical Society, Mystic Seaport, University of Rhode Island, Hazel Webster Wood, Steve Nichols, Sandy Avery, Jim Buffum, David Husband, Mario and Linda Celico, Clifton Woodmansee, Raymond and Arlene Bader, Ellyn Santiago, and the *Westerly Sun*.

The information for the captions came from many different sources. News articles from 1888 to 1910 were most useful. Other useful resources include *Changing Focus*, by Alecia Swasy; *Conservation of Photographs*, by the Eastman Kodak Company; *Currier and Ives America*, edited by Colin Simkin; *Driftway Into the Past*, by the Richmond Historical Society; *Historic and Architectural Resources of Charlestown, R. I.*, by the Rhode Island Historical Preservation Commission; *History of the Town of Hopkinton R. I.: 1757–1976*; *History of Washington & Kent Counties*, by J. R. Cole; *Hope Valley Revived* (The Recorded Past: Photographs & Oral History); *Hopkinton*, by Kirk W. House; *Hopkinton City: The Williamsburg of Hopkinton, Rhode Island*, by Hope Greene Andrews and Patty Andrews; *The Story of Kodak*, by Douglas Collins; *Watch Hill*, by Brigid M. Rooney; *Water Power Revisited*, by Gladys Segar and Betty Salomon; and *The Weekapaug Inn*, by Robert Buffum.

INTRODUCTION

Washington County as we know it today was called King's County during His Majesty's rule. The boundaries lay within the territory of the mighty Narragansett, Niantic, and Pequot tribes, or what was known as Narragansett Country. Throughout the king's rule, the controversies relating to the jurisdiction, possession, and extent of Narragansett Country were abundant. The Revolutionary War brought an end to the king's reign and signaled a new beginning for the people of New England. Many reminders of past sovereign rule were quickly wiped away. At this time, the territory known as King's County was renamed Washington County in honor of our first president, George Washington. It is here in Washington County that Walter Rogers, a talented photographer, chronicled our local history.

Walter Rogers (1856–1927) lived during the time of the Industrial Revolution. His parents were William S. Rogers and Mary Elizabeth, daughter of Russell Thayer. He moved to Westerly when he was a young boy. He went to school in Westerly and then continued his education in New York City, where his photographic talents and artistic abilities were perfected. Rogers later worked in Rochester, New York, with George Eastman, who went on to found the Eastman Kodak Company.

George Eastman was a pioneer in the development of the photographic process, and in 1879, he obtained a patent in London for an emulsion coating machine. The process applied a gelatin emulsion onto a glass plate. This emulsion remained sensitive after drying and could be exposed at leisure. An American patent was granted the following year. Even though the dry-plate photographic method was in use for many years prior to 1879, Eastman improved upon the gelatin emulsion formula and a machine that applied the emulsion. This resulted in a plate that could be produced in mass and of good quality and uniformity. This production process reduced the cost and made photography affordable to many amateurs who found the field of photography too costly a pursuit or hobby.

In New York, Rogers developed his skill as a photoengraver by working with Frederick Ives. Photoengraving is a process of photographic reproduction by which a relief printing surface is obtained for letterpress printing. Photoengraving is much like lithography in which a picture, writing, or the like is applied with grease or an oily substance to a specially prepared stone. An ink impression is then taken from the stone, as in ordinary printing. Lithography was the most common form of photography in the early 1800s.

Nathaniel Currier and James Merrit Ives of Currier and Ives produced many famous prints. Their combined talents brought the art of lithography to its pinnacle in the mid- to late 1800s. The value of an original Currier and Ives print is based on several factors. Scarcity and variation found in prints bearing the same title could account for a print to be valued in the thousands of dollars.

Any work Rogers might have done on lithographic prints is unknown, but it is known that in his later years, he created designs for engraved bonds, certificates, and other legal documents. His work is said to have been meticulous. Examples of the artistic talent of Walter Rogers can be seen on page 60.

Many of the pictures in this book are of Rogers's hometown, the village of Hope Valley. Rogers deemed his life in a small village quite noteworthy. The pictures exhibited in this book are a fraction of his work. It is known that Rogers photographed well over 1,000 images using the dry-plate method of photography and that much of his work throughout Washington County has gone uncredited.

In the early spring of 2005, I visited Hope Valley Antiques, operated by Sandy Avery and Stephen Nichols. They showed me a collection of glass-plate negatives that Steve had purchased at an auction in Connecticut. Prior to this, the glass-plate negatives sat in an old barn undisturbed for decades. Steve, obviously seeing the subject matter (Washington County), felt he had to acquire the negatives and bring them back to Rhode Island. In our discussion and examination of the plates, we discussed the best way to preserve and share this interesting find. I acquired the plates and set off on a mission. With the help of some local historians, it was determined that this was a collection of the work of photographer Walter Rogers. It is interesting to think that Steve's shop was the very place that Rogers had his hardware store and photographic shop some 100 years prior. Thanks to Steve and his foresight, a bit of our past has been preserved.

—Joseph P. Soares

One

COMMUNITY

When Walter Rogers (pictured) was a small boy, his family moved to Westerly, and there he attended school. He continued his education in New York City, and it was in this city that he developed his photographic talents. In the late 1870s, he worked in the company of George Eastman of the Eastman Kodak Company. Later, he worked with Frederick Ives, assisting in perfecting the process of photoengraving.

In the town of Westerly, a young lady stops to pose for the camera. People who lived in the rural parts of Washington County found it necessary to make the trip to larger towns such as Westerly, where many shops offered a greater variety of goods to choose from.

Nellie Nichols (seated in back) was the daughter of Charles S. and Mary (Matteson) Nichols. Charles Nichols was born in 1838 and served valiantly in the battles of Yorktown, Williamsburg, Slatersville, Mechanicsville, Fair Oaks, Malvern Hill, Second Bull Run, Antietam, Williamsport, Fredericksburg (second and third engagements), Gettysburg, Funkstown, Rappahannock Station, Mine Run, and the Wilderness. During the Civil War, Nichols belonged to the 2nd Rhode Island Regiment.

Alice and Stuart Rogers were the children of Walter and Lillie (Nichols) Rogers.

Abbie Greene lived in the village of Hope Valley all her life. Her father, George E. Greene, was the village druggist in Hope Valley.

For many young men, baseball was a favorite pastime—when not doing chores.

May Nichols gathers raspberries. Many people enjoyed harvesting huckleberries. Families and friends would gather at one of the many berry patches throughout the county. It was not uncommon for the day's harvest to be consumed prior to the return home.

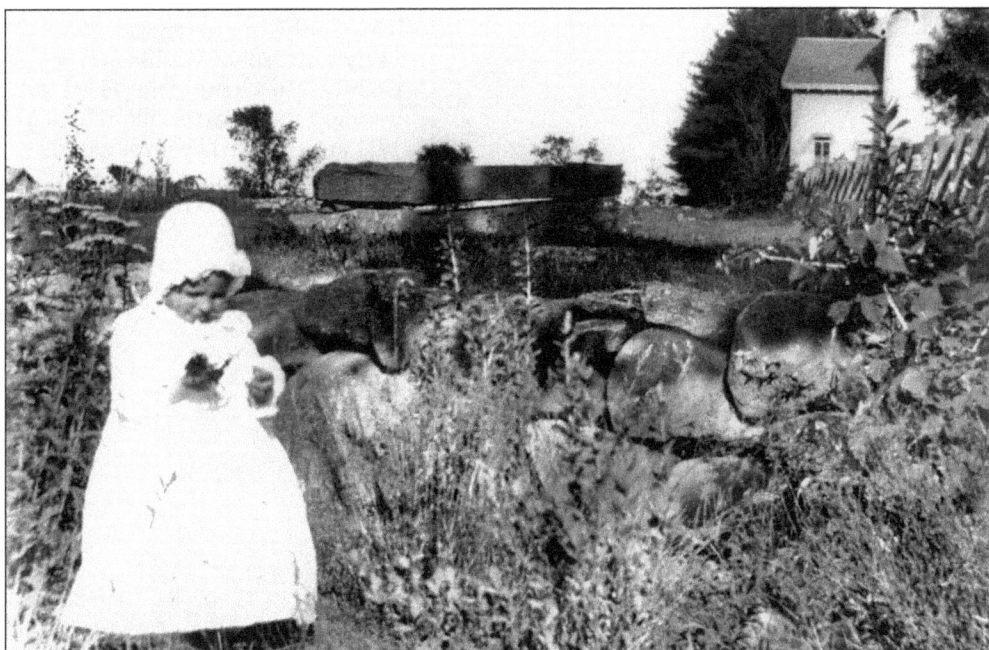

A young lady picks wildflowers on the top of Main Street Hill (Turn Pike Hill) in Hope Valley. For several days in the winter of 1894, many people indulged in coasting on Turn Pike Hill. Three large doublers with heavy loads of young men and maidens made a pretty sight as they went whizzing down the long hill.

Lillian (Nichols) Rogers was the daughter of Silas Nichols Jr. Silas Nichols Jr. was the son of Silas Nichols Sr., who was the brother of Gardner Nichols.

This Civil War veteran was most likely a resident of Washington County. The Grand Army Flag Day was held at the Barberville School in 1911 and observed by guest speaker Rev. John Jerue. Jerue spoke of enlisting as a young man and meeting Abraham Lincoln.

William Woodmansee (front center) was born on January 23, 1825, in Hopkinton and spent much of his life in Rockville, where he was a member of the Rockville Church. In a *Westerly Sun* article, Woodmansee remembers seeing the April 19, 1873, railroad wreck at Wood River Junction, visiting the centennial at Philadelphia in October 1876, and visiting Montreal, Canada, in 1880.

Henry C. Nichols is closest to the camera in this picture. On August 22, 1893, it was reported that the rocks and dunes along the shore at Noyes Beach were dotted with people watching the big breakers. The waves were a grand sight, and when the sun broke through the clouds, it tinted the spray with the colors of the rainbow. It was reported to be too beautiful to describe.

Henry C. Nichols was the treasurer of the Nichols and Langworthy Machine Company. His father was Gardner Nichols.

This is most likely a baptism in Wood River. The ordinance of baptism was administered to the candidates in the Wood River near the Wood River Baptist Church. Rev. D. L. Bennett was the officiating clergyman of many baptisms performed here around 1900.

Amos G. Nichols was the elder son of Capt. Gardner Nichols, one of the founders of the former Nichols and Langworthy Machine Company.

Bicycling along the shores of Westerly became a part of many people's weekend activities. The bicycle also became the primary form of transportation for many villagers around 1900 due in part to better road conditions throughout the county.

Peleg Matteson was a well-known farmer in Hope Valley. His wife, Hannah (Barber) Matteson, was the daughter of Col. Edward and Phebe (Tillinghast) Barber. Born on March 2, 1823, she lived to be 101 years of age.

Mary (Arnold) Nichols was the wife of Amos G. Nichols. She was the daughter of Gorton W. and Nancy (Brown) Arnold and was born on September 30, 1830, in the Old Red House on High Street in the village of Hope Valley. Throughout her life, she was active in church affairs, having joined the Hope Valley Baptist Church at age 19.

Charles Greene was the local druggist in Hope Valley around 1900. His father was George E. Greene, who opened the first drugstore in the village on March 16, 1867, in the former Washington Trust Building. The building, which was also known as Barber Hall, is now the home of Hope Valley Antiques.

The gentleman in the center is Charles Greene of Hope Valley. Bicycling became very popular in Washington County in the late 1800s, and in August 1894, the Ninigret Cycle Club was formed. William M. Chipman was president elect, and John J. Greene was vice president. Bicycling increased in popularity so dramatically that in the village of Wyoming, the number of bicycles rose to around 120 from two dozen in 1897.

19

This photograph was likely taken sometime between 1880 and 1889 in Washington County. The children seem at ease while having their picture taken.

Pictured here is Charles Greene. His drugstore in the village of Hope Valley sold many items. In early March 1911, young Frank Fish purchased a resplendent kite from Greene. Securing a No. 8 thread, he started out, but suddenly the string broke and the kite sailed gracefully away over the village. Finally, the thread was caught in the trees by Wood River and attracted much attention. The kite remained flying all night long and into the next day until it freed itself and flew gracefully away over Richmond.

The woman on the left is Mary Champlin Greene, wife of George E. Greene. George E. Greene operated the drugstore in the village of Hope Valley. The baby is Lester Nichols Greene, and the boy to the right is his older brother, Channcey E. Greene.

The employees of the Nichols and Langworthy Machine Company were highly skilled in their profession. On June 13, 1894, several students from the State Agricultural College were given a tour of the shop and various departments. About three hours were spent watching special machines that manufactured steam engines. The visitors expressed surprise at finding in a small country village a plant so well equipped.

Two

DWELLINGS

The Hezekiah Carpenter house was built in 1770 on Main Street in Hope Valley. This was the birthplace of Prudence Crandall, born on September 3, 1803. Around 1900, the residence was known as the Ray house. Isaiah Ray was a retired sea captain, and it is said that youngsters from the village would go to his house and ride on the giant sea turtle kept behind the house.

Built around 1841, the Josiah Langworthy house is located on Mechanic Street in Hope Valley, overlooking the Nichols and Langworthy Machine Shop. Josiah Langworthy was well respected, and in 1843, he represented the town in the state senate, thus becoming a member of the first legislature. This group assembled under the Constitution, recently adopted to supersede the charter granted by Charles II in 1666. Langworthy was a strong advocate of temperance and the abolition of slavery.

This is the W. R. Greene house in Hope Valley. In the late 1800s, a series of street lanterns were lit throughout the fall and winter months, except on bright moonlit evenings. In 1895, the town exhausted its funds for streetlights, resulting in total darkness in the village. Many townspeople thought the system was ineffectual anyway and carried on as normal.

This gambrel-roofed house was located on Mechanic Street in Hope Valley. It was built in 1778 by Ethan Clark, who ran an ironworks close by. Young Prudence Crandall moved into this house with her parents, Pardon and Esther (Carpenter) Crandall. In 1831, at the age of 28, Prudence Crandall founded a school in Canterbury, Connecticut. A pioneer educator, she advocated the education of black children.

The Amos G. Nichols house, built around 1870, sat high on the hill overlooking the mill complex of the Nichols and Langworthy Machine Company. Amos G. Nichols was president of the company around 1900.

Mary and Amos Nichols entertained frequently at their home. In 1899, the annual meeting of the Farther Lights Mission was held at their residence. A social hour followed the meeting. Refreshments were served, singing was encouraged, and Willis Nichols played a selection on the gramophone.

Built around 1829, the Almon Godfrey house, on Mechanic Street in Hope Valley, is one of the older houses in the village. In 1810, there were only two houses in the village. John Godfrey, Godfrey Arnold, Gorton Arnold, and others purchased a large tract of land and built a third house known as the Big House.

The Rowland Hiscox house, located on the corner of Main and High Streets, is one of the older houses in the village of Hope Valley. The village roads were for the most part maintained by the United Village Improvement Association. The association was a group of volunteers who put in sidewalks, planted and trimmed the elms on Main Street, installed street lanterns, and accomplished other tasks of that nature.

The Crandall house is located on Main Street in Hope Valley. In 1909, the state road from Ashaway to Hope Valley was completed. Many people complained that speeding automobiles were tearing up the new roadbed. A speed limit of 15 miles per hour had been in place, but many thought that this was much too fast a speed to travel.

This photograph was taken in front of the Crandall house. The man in the buggy is most likely Mr. Crandall. The village of Canonchet is located near this house. On a winter day in 1898, Nathan Noble and Mr. Briggs rode to this village to purchase a small pig, which they placed in a bag in the back of the wagon. Briggs prided himself on having a fast horse and a superior buggy, and being in a hurry that day, he drove home rapidly. Noble, the owner of the new pig, called to his wife to come see their new squealer, but upon reaching the back of the wagon they discovered that the bag and the pig were gone. Mrs. Noble and Briggs laughed, but Nathan Noble cried out that the pig was unusually smart. The two hurried back to retrieve what they had lost. At the conclusion of this trying event, Noble exclaimed that he would never again attempt to move a pig in a bag.

The Gardner Nichols home, built around 1840, is located on Mechanic Street near the Nichols and Langworthy Machine Shop. Gardiner Nichols was man of strong religious convictions and a devoted member of the Baptist church throughout his life.

This is the Thomas H. Greene house on Main Street. In the late 1800s, Capt. Thomas H. Greene was employed as boss farmer for the Nichols and Langworthy Machine Company.

The Barber house, on the corner of Bank Street and Fairview Avenue, was built in 1863. In the mid-1930s, a room on the third floor served as a schoolroom for the town's kindergartners.

The David L. Aldrich house on High Street was built around 1860. David L. Aldrich was instrumental in the construction of the Wood River Branch Railroad, of which he was president for many years.

This image was taken from what was Hill Street in Hope Valley. The house on the left is where Prudence Crandall lived when she was a young girl. The house to the right of that was known as the Big House. The Big House was first occupied as a residence by Capt. Gardner Nichols and his partners. His son, Amos G. Nichols, was born in this house. It was later converted into a tenement house and was subsequently destroyed by fire in 1909.

The Gorton W. Arnold house, also known as the Old Red House, was built around 1840. It was located next to the Waverly House on High Street. This was the first house built on what some called the Arnold Triangle.

The Benjamin Langworthy house is located on Main Street in Hope Valley. Main Street was used by the Park Brother Auto Line, established in 1909, to drive villagers from Hope Valley by automobile to Ashaway. There, they could take the trolley to Westerly. The auto line was said to be very useful on days when the train from Depot Square was not in service.

Orville M. Meserve lived in this house on the corner of Maple and Main Streets in Hope Valley. In November 1897, a surprise party was held in Meserve's honor for his devoted service to the Hope Valley Grange, of which he was an officer during this flourishing period of the Grange. It is said that Mrs. Meserve served oysters for part of the feast and that people passed the time with games and songs.

This picture, taken around 1870, features the home of Henry C. Nichols. It is located on the corner of Main Street and Nichols Lane in the village of Hope Valley. Henry Nichols was the son of Gardner Nichols. Prior to 1894, Main Street was known as the New London Turnpike. At its annual meeting in March 1894, the United Village Improvement Association decided to name and in some cases rename the streets of the village.

The Jordan house is located on Main Street in Hope Valley. Note the closed shutters. On a Saturday in July 1894, a tempest passed over the village and milkman William Lillibridge reported that the storm was so severe at his place that farm implements were blown around. His hired hand, who was also blown about, lay on the ground and clung to the grass until the storm went by.

The Jedediah D. Witter house stands on Main Street next to the Hezekiah Carpenter house in Hope Valley. It was built around 1873. Jedediah D. Witter was the son of Josiah and Dorcas Witter. He was born on March 6, 1817.

A row of old houses once stood on the high hill that was located just before the Barberville Dam, heading toward Arcadia.

Three

OCEAN AND SHORE

This picture was taken from a tugboat in September 1913. It shows the setting of huge granite slabs along the shore in front of the Weekapaug Inn, for protection from the waves. The granite slabs came from the quarries of Westerly. The boat was named the *Richard*.

The Quonacontaug Life Saving Station was built around 1900. In 1901, the local resorts could accommodate 1,800 to 2,000 visitors on a summer Sunday. Visitors came from all directions and in all sorts of conveyances. Every craft capable of getting people to Watch Hill and the beaches was pressed into service. The lifesaving station was a necessity year-round.

Quonacontaug was a popular retreat for those seeking rest and relaxation. The Eldridge House in Quonacontaug, the Larken House in Watch Hill, and the Weekapaug Inn in Weekapaug were just a few places of retreat in the area.

In 1899, amongst the dunes, the Weekapaug Inn was built. Weekapaug grew every year, as more cottages were built, and the area soon became a shore destination. In 1903, plans were made to enlarge the inn, which more than doubled in size.

Many inland villagers would make the long trip to the shore. The allure of the fresh salt air and the tranquility of the beaches made the trip worthwhile.

The rocky shore at Weekapaug made beachcombing a challenge. Note the naval ships in the background. On August 18, 1903, a ceremony and naval review was held off the coast of New York for Pres. Theodore Roosevelt. The ceremony was reported to be magnificent, and the president was said to be impressed.

Beside the huge granite slabs placed along the shore, piles were also driven into the ground, which afforded some protection from the waves. This, however, was not enough. The Hurricane of 1938 destroyed the Old Weekapaug Inn. A new inn was built high and dry on a new site. By the end of June 1939, the inn was once again ready for guests.

Bathing attire, often referred to as costumes at the time, came in several styles. Sailor collars were one feature often seen on women's costumes. Knee pants and quarter-sleeve shirts were the most common style for men.

Along the sandy dunes to the east of the Weekapaug Inn, many new cottages were built at the dawn of the 20th century.

This building was known as the Fishing Shanty at Noyes Beach to those who visited the shore resorts in the 1890s.

These pictures show local farmers harvesting seaweed at Wiquapaug. Seaweed was widely used as fertilizer. Within days after a storm, farmers made the journey to the beach by horse and wagon to collect what Mother Nature brought ashore.

Bathers enjoy the surf on the beach in front of the Weekapaug Inn. To fit in more naturally amongst the dunes, the inn was built in a Colonial style.

This picture was taken at Noyes Beach. On the left is Henry C. Nichols. It was reported in the local newspaper that on September 28, 1893, Herbert Taylor left Noyes Beach by bicycle for town but came back on foot. In an effort to avoid two teams of horses while coasting down Granite Street, he collided with a picket fence. He badly crushed the front wheel of the bicycle but was fortunate to escape unhurt.

The Ashaway was a group of cottages at Quonacontaug.

Known simply as the Log Cabin, this building was situated next to the Taylor cottage west of the Weekapaug Inn. The cabin was a well-known landmark to the many visitors of Weekapaug. It was swept away during the Hurricane of 1938.

The small cottage of Amos Nichols sat behind the main cottage at Weekapaug. Many socials were held there.

Bathers stroll the beach, heading for the Weekapaug Inn. The back of the inn faces Quonacontaug Pond and its picturesque shoreline.

Shown is the original Briars Cottage in Weekapaug in the early 1890s.

The original cottage was destroyed by fire. Pictured around 1910 is the Briars Cottage after being rebuilt by Leon Bliven.

The Taylor cottage was just west of the Weekapaug Inn. It was swept away during the Hurricane of 1938.

Shown here is a scene from around 1906. The cottage on the left belonged to Henry C. Nichols. The cottage next to that belonged to Amos G. Nichols. Behind Amos Nichols's cottage was a smaller cottage where many guests enjoyed the summer days at Weekapaug.

Two fair maidens examine a strange object at Quonacontaug Pond. Weekapaug Day was held on August 30, 1906, and a water carnival took place on the waters of Quonacontaug Pond. A prize was awarded for the best decorated boat. Canoe races and many other events took place throughout the day.

The Larkin house is situated on Light House Point in Watch Hill. The house marketed itself as the destination of choice for the affluent customers. It was built in 1869 with modern conveniences such as gas lighting, telephone, and entertainment. Its popularity grew, and more room was needed. Thus, a substantial addition was built in 1876.

This is known as Spray Rock at Weekapaug. From the looks of this photograph, the name seems appropriate.

Walter Rogers titled this picture "Frosted Rocks at Weekapaug." Many seasonal residents purchased their ice from the Langworthy brother who had a local icehouse. The iceman, as he was called, was a welcome sight during the hot summer months.

Noyes Beach was officially changed to Weekapaug in July 1899. For two seasons or more, there was a post office known as Noyes Beach located at the Chapman farmhouse, which sat back from the beach.

Four

FOLKLORE AND

VILLAGE LIFE

The Odd Fellows Block was built in 1874 by the Independent Order of Odd Fellows, Mechanic's Lodge No. 14. Prior to 1874, the members met in various places and were described as the Children of Israel in search of their home. They wanted to settle in one place, and that long cherished desire was fulfilled in the year 1874. A building was erected, and the hall was consecrated with impressive ceremonies to the principles of friendship, love, and truth. The Ark of Covenant was safely placed upon the altar in the temple. In building this beautiful structure, the members incurred a heavy debt, but the Odd Fellows had confidence in their growth and ability to meet these obligations. With determination and hard work, their aspirations came true and the lodge's debt was canceled and the evidence burned during a well-attended meeting in 1895.

On July 29, 1897, lightning struck the Odd Fellows Block in several places. Discoveries were made throughout the following day of places where the lightning had left its impression. The library rooms were damaged, the covers of the chimney smoke flues were blown out, and the telephone box in the T. B. Segar and Company grocery store was damaged on the cover. Also, the stairs at the west end of the building were split open.

In 1895, extensive improvements were made to the Odd Fellows Block. Additional space was made for the Langworthy Public Library, and new bookcases were put in place. The Langworthy Public Library was located in the Odd Fellows Block, as was the *Hope Valley Advertiser* newspaper and T. B. Segar and Company grocery store.

54

This picture was labeled "Tally Ho Kingstown Fair." The carriage was built for comfort and elegance. A carriage of this size would be drawn by two to four horses and could transport a large group with ease.

During the week of the county fair, many of the local mills would shut down to afford their employees a chance to relax and spend time with their families and friends. Many schoolchildren residing in Washington County participated in the activities and events that the annual fair offered.

This young man (singing) is most likely participating in one of the contests held during the fair. Besides the many contests, there were exhibits, amusements, horse races, bicycle races, restaurants, the midway, freaks, and entertainment.

This large hall was used at the Kingstown Fair to hold indoor activities and exhibits. For the many visitors to the fair in 1897, the Boston Zoo, which was at the east end of the fairgrounds, was the first stop. It is said to have been the finest and most deserving place of amusement. On the second day of the fair, five baby lions were born. Surely this event was an honor and a first for Kingstown.

Camping with family and friends provided unforgettable and cherished memories. Many of the exploits that occurred during a weekend camping trip furnished interesting conversation at the dinner table. Just imagine the story behind "Hobo's Retreat."

A short distance from here along the shoreline of Stonington, Captain Chesebros first saw the sea monster that swam along the coast. Later, Charles Smith and Thomas Harty nearly snared the beast at Potter's Cove. But the sea monster was captured at Prudence Island in early December 1908.

Capture of the "Goroo" at Prudence Island

The serpent was captured at Prudence Island and brought ashore and examined by several versed in natural history. Some thought it to be a goroo, but others disagreed. The creature was estimated to weigh a ton and a half, and it had two large flippers and eyes the size of an alarm clock. The islanders used all sorts of pointed implements to prod the animal and move it along. This depiction was printed in the *Providence Journal* in December 1908.

Walter Rogers was not only a talented photographer but also an artist. Pictured are album covers he created for the Postal Photographic Club.

This scene, with its open pastures and rolling hills, was common of many farms in Washington County. Few remember when dynamite was used regularly on the farm. The Dupont Powder Company gave a practical demonstration of the use of dynamite in farm operations in Kingston in April 1911. The demonstration covered the use of dynamite for cultivating, blasting boulders, aeration, and drainage.

Readiness in helping one's neighbor was a common trait in most villages. In June 1895, E. M. Smith, who lived a short distance south of the village, lost her valuable cow after it expired from eating wild cherry leaves. A paper was circulated among the employees of the Nichols and Langworthy Machine Company, and a sum of $16 was raised for the purchase of another cow for the poor woman.

The town clock at the Nichols and Langworthy Machine Company was quite large and would ring on the hour. It could be heard for miles in all directions. On occasions during severe winter storms, the hands on the clock would become heavily incrusted with snow, stopping the mechanism. The villagers who did not possess a watch relied heavily on the town clock and listened instinctively for the hourly ring.

This may not be Coward's Hole, but it surely looked very similar to the place Captain Kidd chose to store his stolen treasures. Two accounts dating from before 1900 refer to Kidd's treasure. The reports state that the daring sea robber picked the hills and valleys of Richmond. Sometime during the 16th century, the gold, silver, and other valuables were brought ashore on what is now Charlestown Beach and hauled overland to be buried at a point south of the old Turnpike Road in the dense woods of Richmond, a dismal place called Coward's Hole.

Dogs are man's best friend, but a cat named Tom took top billing at the Nichols and Langworthy Machine Company. On April 3, 1894, it was reported in the local newspaper that Tom, the famous old shop cat and a general favorite with the workmen in the shop, fell over dead. Tom had become a fixture at the shop. He was a notorious rat catcher and was much liked for his amiable disposition.

The traveling circus brought great joy to the many villages throughout Washington County. It is said that villagers would line the street and would watch anxiously as the circus wagons, animals, and performers passed through town.

Family farms were numerous around 1900. Children were relied upon to a great extent in the day-to-day operation of the farm.

Five

CHURCHES AND SCHOOLS

The Methodist Episcopal Church was erected in Rockville in the year 1846. In 1851, the church was disassembled and brought to the village of Hope Valley, where it was reassembled on Main Street. In the early 1900s, the church became inactive and the property was sold to the Roman Catholic Diocese in Providence. The original church building was all but destroyed in the Hurricane of 1938.

The First Baptist Church of Hope Valley was first organized in December 1841. A place of worship, celebration, and mourning, this enduring landmark was an essential part of daily life for many in the village.

Photographer Walter Rogers was a devoted member of the First Baptist Church of Hope Valley. He served the church as a clerk for a short time prior to 1889. He also served on the Hope Valley School Board of Trustees in 1894.

This is the Hope Valley First Baptist Church parsonage, built in 1891. The cost to construct and to partially furnish the dwelling was about $3,000. That same year, a front vestibule was added to the church.

A gathering was held around 1900 at the Hope Valley Baptist Church to honor the veterans of the Grand Army of the Republic.

In 1880, as a memorial to his wife, Gardner Nichols provided the Hope Valley Baptist Church with this grand pipe organ. New stained-glass windows were later installed in the church in December 1899. Rev. E. I. Lindh delivered the dedicatory sermon.

This photograph was taken inside the First Baptist Church in Hope Valley prior to December 1899, when the stained-glass windows were installed. The young ladies probably belong to the choir or helped with Sunday school.

Many of Walter Rogers's photographs are of buildings of historic or religious importance. He took this photograph of the Indian Church in Charlestown around 1900.

Walter Rogers wrote on the sleeve of this glass-plate negative, "Ninigret Lodge." The site of the Indian Schoolhouse and Ninigret Lodge was situated along the north end of Quacumpaug Pond (later Schoolhouse Pond) in Charlestown. The original Indian Schoolhouse was built in 1745. Around 1815, the old schoolhouse was replaced by another and named the Narragansett Indian Schoolhouse.

This was the schoolhouse on Main Street in Hope Valley. In 1897, the villagers of Hope Valley, dealing with the increasing number of new students and the crowded old single-story schoolhouse, found it necessary to find additional classroom space. Architect L. P. Langworthy of Providence was hired to draw up plans. The solution was to raise the existing single-story schoolhouse and add a new first floor.

"Hickory, dickory, dock, the mouse ran down the bell rope." This old nursery rhyme with a twist was heard in the school yard on an April day in 1896. A mouse made his presence known just as Miss Wheeler, the schoolteacher, was going to ring the school bell for noonday intermission. The event caused quit a ripple of excitement among the young ladies.

This image, labeled "Soldier Monument," was taken around 1900. The many monuments dedicated to fallen soldiers were gracefully decorated during village celebrations such as the Fourth of July and Memorial Day. Members of the local Grand Army of the Republic post would decorate the many scattered graves of veterans. According to reports, it would often be nearly dark before the last grave was decorated.

Located in the Pine Grove Cemetery is the Barber Memorial Tomb, which was built with walls 14 inches thick and a 10- by 10-foot vestibule anteroom. The tomb was presented to the Pine Grove Cemetery Association by the Honorable Edward Barber in commemoration of his 80th birthday on August 3, 1897. It was reported that the rooms, so pleasant and cheerfully finished, had little appearance of a tomb. The anteroom was used to hold services for the deceased in inclement weather.

Six

TRANSPORTATION

The Wood River Branch Railroad began service in 1874 and soon became a vital source of transportation for the area's growing population. There were several locomotives in service during the time of operation. Some engines were named after people and places, such as the *Gardiner Nichols*, the *Wincheck*, and the *Polly*. The only identifying mark on this engine is "WRBRR 5." There was also reported to be a locomotive named the *Cinderella*, which started service in the spring of 1911.

Pawcamet Lake, also known as Beach Pond, was a very popular destination throughout the summer months. On an August day in 1894, an estimated 1,500 to 2,000 people gathered along the shore. Representation from such villages as Wyoming, Hope Valley, Rockville, Voluntown, Jewett City, Plainfield, Highland, and Preston assembled. Activities included swimming, boating, singing, dancing, dining, and a fine selection of games for the youths and maidens in attendance.

A passenger coach similar to this one at Depot Square rolled over on a cold December morning in 1904. The mishap occurred when a Wood River Branch Railroad train derailed on its way to the junction near the covered bridge over Wood River. There were 10 passengers in the coach when it rolled over, and luckily no one was seriously injured.

The gentleman standing on this footbridge is identified as John. This footbridge crossed Wood River along the wooded path known as the String Piece. This path started in Hope Valley and ended at Reynolds Cards sheep pasture in Wyoming. Many of the villagers living in Wyoming used the path to walk to work in Hope Valley.

On a Friday evening in December 1895, a train was passing by this railroad crossing at the Nichols and Langworthy Machine Company. A coupling pin broke, leaving the passenger train standing still. The locomotive, called the *Gardner Nichols*, and a number of freight cars continued traveling, but a glance backward by engineer Nichols revealed a vigorous lantern signal from brakeman Gardner. The train was quickly reunited and once again went on its way.

Throughout the summer months, many socials were held at the various cottages along the shore. In the 1890s, shoregoers from inland villages would arrive by means of Lester's Big Party Wagon, which was drawn by six horses. The party wagon was also employed to convey the local brass bands to and from various engagements.

Pictured in the rear of the buggy is the Reverend and Mrs. E. L. Lindh. Reverend Lindh became pastor of Hope Valley Baptist Church in November 1898. A cordial reception was held in the middle of November at the church to welcome the new pastor.

On a cool summer day, a ride in an open carriage was pleasurable. But in inclement weather, a carriage with a top was a savior. The driver looks to be holding a torch, which might be used if darkness fell while en route.

On October 8, 1894, Phebe Babcock lost control of her carriage. It was described as a meteor coming down Spring Street from Moscow. The horse, said to be a hard-bitten animal, could not make the corner and overturned the carriage. Phebe Babcock and her mother spilled into Depot Square by the River View Cottage, fortunately without serious injury. It is said the horse and carriage continued up Main Street, minus the rear wheels.

Mrs. Langworthy and company prepare to take a delightful carriage ride through the village. The house in the background is the Benjamin Langworthy house, on Main Street in the village of Hope Valley.

When the horseless carriage first arrived, most villagers thought it to be a novelty. The price of this new contraption was not affordable for the average person.

Young Willis Gardner Nichols enjoys a pony ride along the shore at Noyes Beach. On August 22, 1893, it was reported in the local newspaper that a tent was pitched by three lads at Noyes Beach on what is known as the Big Island. They brought their tent, equipment, and other provisions in a handcart from Westerly. The journey took four hours, and the cart was seen stuck in the mud at one point.

Pictured is Henry C. Nichols driving his car in Weekapaug. Nichols lived on the corner of Main Street and Nichols Lane in the village of Hope Valley. This was one of a few automobiles seen on a regular basis in the village after 1900. After Nichols stopped driving, the car sat undisturbed for many years in the barn beside his house.

A Sunday morning ride in a motor carriage was always an adventure. The gentleman on the right is Benjamin P. Langworthy II, who resided on Turn Pike Hill (Main Street) in Hope Valley. Langworthy enjoyed farming and was well respected in the village.

Many children learned to ride at an early age. These two young people seem at ease upon the horse of Amos G. Nichols, while Mrs. A. G. Nichols leads them along.

Valued as a work animal but stubborn at times, the mule was the animal of choice for many villagers.

The horse and buggy was once the popular form of transportation. In early August 1898, flying horses were seen in the village of Hope Valley. Traveling penny catchers had set up a tent pavilion, which contained flying horses driven by steam, at the northern end of town. It was reported that the flying horse company was raking in the nickels. A dime museum in the big tent also drew a large crowd.

Seven

WATERFALLS AND MILLS

The Nichols and Langworthy Machine Shop, located at the foot of Mechanic Street in Hope Valley, built steam engines and boilers. The steam engines and boilers were shipped throughout the country and were used in many different applications such as the power source to run dynamos to furnish electricity. They were also used as the main source of power for the many new mills being built across the country.

This is a picturesque view of the Nichols and Langworthy Machine Company. On February 14, 1899, it was reported that Henry C. Nichols of Hope Valley patented a new type of steam engine governor. The engineering description of the patent was quite impressive, and this new governor advanced the efficiency and safety of the steam boilers manufactured at the company.

On April 13, 1909, a fire broke out at the Nichols and Langworthy Machine Company just before noon. The flames spread rapidly throughout the mill complex, and by 1:30 p.m., the machine shop was a mass of ruins. The fire also spread across the street to dwelling houses and other structures, burning many of these to the ground. It was perhaps started by an explosion in the dock gasoline building. This building housed several big gasoline engines that were set up and ready for delivery to the federal government.

This is a photograph of the Hope Valley Dam. To the left is Hopkinton, and to the right is Richmond. The mills on both sides of the river ran year-round. In the winter months, anchor ice would accumulate in the wheel pit, hindering the wheel's movement and causing much of the machinery in the mills to stop. Eventually the ice would be dislodged and power restored.

The Niantic Dyeing Company is pictured around 1903. It was owned by the Niantic and Phoenix Bank, located in what is now Bradford. The mill was sold to the Bradford Dyeing Association of England around 1910. Many improvements and additional manufacturing space was added shortly thereafter. In April 1911, a bill was introduced to the Rhode Island legislature to change the name of the village from Niantic to Bradford.

Pictured is the Niantic Mill. The village of Niantic had been called many different names over the years. The oldest designation of the place was Shattuck's Weir. Shattuck was the name of an Indian closely associated with this area's early history.

The building to the left is the Locustville Mill. The mill was once used for the manufacture of woolen and other goods. The first dam and mill at this site were built around 1814. A series of fires changed the appearance of the mill over the years.

The Locustville Mill is pictured around 1870.

This image shows the Locustville Mill after a fire. Note the roofline of the main building.

The Wyoming Dam looks much the same today as it did when this photograph was taken in 1890. The building on the left, which was on the Hope Valley side of the river, is gone now.

Pictured is the intake gate mechanism, which controlled the amount of water going to the wheel. This intake was located on the Hope Valley side of the Wyoming Dam.

Centerville Mill, located just past the Twin Ponds, was built around 1865 just downstream from Rockville. The building was built of brick with much detail. Originally there was a bell in the tower said to have belonged to John Paul Jones, the famous U.S. Navy sea admiral. The bell's location now is a mystery. A disastrous fire severely damaged the mill on April 7, 1947. The building was rebuilt and is still in use today.

Pictured is the Wyoming Dam around 1890. To the right are Wyoming and the Sheldon Mill. The main portion of the mill complex was built by John Olney in 1846 to replace an existing structure that was destroyed by fire. In 1897, the American Mica Company started refining mica at this site. Mica was shipped in its crude form from mines in New Hampshire and Canada.

The building in the middle of this picture was once used as a company store and boardinghouse for workers of Taylor Manufacturing and the Nichols and Langworthy Machine Company. The building to the far right is the Taylor Manufacturing Company. The building with the clock tower, to the left, is the Nichols and Langworthy Mill, located on the other side of the river in Hope Valley.

The Wyoming Mill was located just before the bridge that connects Hope Valley and Wyoming. Just down the road was the Orrin Deady Saloon. On a cold February night in 1910, a horse and buggy was stolen from the shed in the rear of the saloon. The next day, Deputy Sheriff G. Barber apprehended the thiefs many miles away. The deputy reported that the case was easy; he just followed the wagon marks left in the snow.

This was the Taylor Manufacturing Company, later known as the Mystic Mill. A portion of this mill was very old and believed to be the third-oldest cotton manufacturer in the United States.

Moscow Mill was built around 1878. This building replaced one that burned in August 1876. A fire in 1952 and another in 1955 severely damaged the mill.

Railroad ties were in great demand around 1900. This sawmill was located in Washington County, but the exact location is unknown. Many sawmills were portable and moved from one woodlot to another. In the makeshift building pictured here is a small steam boiler, which powered the mill.

The flood of 1886 caused extensive damage to many buildings in low-lying areas. Shown is one of the mill buildings of the Nichols and Langworthy Machine Company during the flood.

The village of Barberville was formed around 1829, when a dam and sawmill were built by Joseph T. Barber. Around 1839, brothers Thomas T. and Edward Barber formed a company named TT &E Barber and engaged in the manufacturing of carriages, coffins, and furniture.

This mill was located somewhere in Washington County. The picture was taken prior to 1900, and by the looks of the waterwheel and the windows, the mill must have sat abandoned for some time.

Eight

STREET SCENES

This is a picturesque view of Hope Valley center behind Depot Square around 1885. In the middle of this picture sits the bandstand. The first floor was used as the town jail. Note the passenger car of the Wood River Branch Railroad at the lower left. Also pictured are large stacks of railroad ties. Railroad ties were a big export for Hope Valley during this period.

The steam whistle was heard several times daily at Depot Square in Hope Valley. The first train began service on July 1, 1874. This was the starting point of many Fourth of July celebrations. Even though the depot is no longer there, local residents still refer to the spot as the Square.

Pictured around 1900 is Dawley Tavern, once a center for town government, musters, and other gatherings. The tavern was also a hostelry for travelers on the New London Turnpike, and in later years it housed a number of small shops. Recent preservation work has brought this historic landmark back to life.

This picture is from Main Street looking down Bank Street in Hope Valley. The second building from the left is the location of S. R. Avery and Company, an undertaking and furniture business, located at the beginning of Bank Street in the village of Hope Valley. On the Fourth of July 1897, the company entered a finely decorated float in the annual street parade. On the wagon was a nice bed containing a dummy with a black mask, representing an invalid, which many spectators thought was a corpse.

This is midday on Maple Street in Hope Valley. The many maple trees still line the road.

This was the bandstand at Depot Square in Hope Valley. It was the spot where many village meetings and celebrations took place. The Baptist church also held outdoor services here when weather permitted. The bottom floor was used as the village jail.

A delivery wagon pauses on Maple Street. An unfortunate occurrence took place at the bottom of High Street on a cold December day in 1893. A horse and buggy driven by Elmer Larkin collided with the milk wagon of William W. Lillibridge. Larkin, not observing the team, struck the milk wagon, wrecking the wheels and spilling a large quantity of milk. His wife was thrown from the buggy, but fortunately she escaped serious injury.

Gasoline engines started showing up in the village of Hope Valley around 1900. Depot Square held perhaps the first gas station in the area. On the right is a small tank with the word "gasolene" printed on it—perhaps the way they spelled gasoline back then.

This photograph of Hope Valley was taken from the cupola atop the Odd Fellows building. The water tower was part of the Locustville Mill complex. To the left is Locustville Pond. Here on December 28, 1897, it was reported that scores of people were enjoying magnificent skating and the icemen were busily engaging in preparation for harvesting ice.

Pictured is the Columbia Brass Band. On November 5, 1896, many villages throughout Washington County celebrated the election of William McKinley as president. In Hope Valley the Nichols and Langworthy Company's old gun used to celebrate victories during the Civil War was brought out. The cannon was drawn along the route to Wyoming by many willing hands, and occasionally it belched forth its deafening roar. About 50 pounds of powder was used along the way.

The building on the left was the house of the foreman of the Locustville Mill in Hope Valley. It is now gone, as are the many elms that lined Main Street at the dawn of the new century.

Main Street in Hope Valley looks a lot different here than it does today. Gone are the many elms and other species of trees that lined the street on both sides.

Pictured is the horse-drawn float of the Nichols and Langworthy Machine Company in the 1899 Fourth of July parade. On the wagon is an engine, boiler, and a small press.

Picturesque views of stone walls and rolling pastures were once common throughout Washington County.

The Hope Valley post office was once in the Arnold Building on the corner of Mechanic and High Streets. It was also the Hope Valley office of the Wood River Branch Railroad and the home of A. M. Bailey grocery market. On Tuesday morning, February 13, 1900, the employees discovered that burglars had entered both offices during the night and blown open both safes. About $40 in stamps was missing, and a packet of valuable paper (not negotiable) was taken from the railroad office. The two explosions did not arouse anyone, and the robbers did not leave the slightest clue behind.

The building to the left is the Odd Fellows Block, now the location of H. C. Woodmansee and Son Oil Company. The building to the right on the other side of Main Street was the Sash and Blind Factory, started by Benjamin P. Langworthy in the 1870s.

At the crest of the hill on Mechanic Street in Hope Valley was the market of F. W. Crandall. The many grocers in the village had delivery wagons that were fully stocked. It was reported in the village of Rockville in 1895 that wagons would appear daily upon the streets, supplying the people with all the necessities of life.

This photograph was taken from the cupola atop the Odd Fellows building, looking up Mechanic Street. The building to the left had a store on the bottom floor and a meeting hall on the upper floor. To the right is the Old Chapman house. The large water tower to the left was erected in August 1893. It was located on the east side of the S. A. Owens Mill in Richmond.

A horse-drawn buggy stops in front of the Baptist church in Hope Valley. The front of the church looks quite different today.

The photograph offers a view of Depot Square in Hope Valley. Note the windmill atop the building to the right. Around 1900, windmills were scatted throughout the land, mostly used for the purpose of pumping water for residential use.

Individuals from the many villages of Washington County would gather to celebrate special occasions. Quaint terms such as Rockvillian, Hope Valleyite, and Westerlyite were used to describe one's hometown.

A. M. Bailey Grocery and Market (left) was located on the bottom floor of the post office building facing Mechanic Street. Benjamin Pendleton had a meat market where Bailey's was at one time. He drove a meat wagon through the villages three times a week. The house behind Bailey facing Mechanic Street is the Joseph Langworthy house, built in 1841.

Nine

SPECIAL PLACES

At the center of Depot Square stood a fountain. In the middle of June 1894, George Nichols, a public-spirited citizen, tapped the underground pipe that supplied the fountain and placed a standing pipe with faucet, cup, and chain. In doing this, pedestrians could slake their thirst without crossing the dusty street crowded with horses and carriages. The water came from a nice cool spring, which was much appreciated.

This is the Old Chipman house on Mechanic Street in Hope Valley. The Langworthy Public Library was located here for a period of time after the Library Association purchased the property in September 1916.

River View Cottage was located next to a hack and livery in Hope Valley. It is said to have been built as a barn by brothers Joshua and Almon Godfrey. It was later converted to a dwelling around 1838. George H. Barber was the proprietor of the River View cottage, which offered comfortable lodgings.

On April 13, 1894, the Washington County Medical Society held a meeting at River View Cottage. The meeting was well attended. Dr. William James of Westerly, the president of the society, presided. After the adjournment, a fine dinner was served to the society by the landlord, George H. Barber. On June 25, 1894, Dr. Cole stopped at River View cottage with an experimental magnetic healing device. Also during that week, salesmen from the Kickapoo Indian Medicine Company held nightly entertainment opposite W. E. Browning's. The Kickapoo Indian medicine men peddled an herbal concoction, which was used to treat many diseases and ailments. It seemed to have been the combination of these very different medical treatments that led to an altercation between the doctor and representatives of the Kickapoo company at one of the open-air gatherings. It was reported in the local newspaper that humbug was exposed.

Pictured is the aftermath of a bank robbery, which only netted the thiefs $6.02. In the early morning of August 14, 1909, the First National Bank in Hope Valley was the target of two robbers. They blew open two bank safes and caused a lot of damage to the bank's interior.

The Waverly House, also known as the Hope Valley Hotel, was located on lower High Street. In the *Wood River Advertiser*, the hotel advertised that it offered superior accommodation for commercial agents and transient or permanent boarders. On many occasions, theater companies stayed at the hotel while they put on shows at Waverly Hall or Barbers Hall. Many of the theater companies would perform in a street parade while en route to Barbers Hall.

This image shows Kenyon Block around 1907. It was on the right as one started up Spring Street from Depot Square. It was occupied by a millinery shop on one side and a five-and-dime store on the other side. At a later date, the A&P grocery store was located in this building.

Many local farmers throughout the villages of Washington County raised cows for beef or milk. These products were used on the farm, and the excess was often sold to local grocers or creameries for further distribution.

In June 1894, burglars entered the Hope Valley post office one night by using a heavy chisel to pry open the front door. A five-eighths-inch hole was drilled in the top of the safe and powder or dynamite was used to blow the doors open. An estimated $15 in stamps, $4 in pennies, and an English sovereign were taken. The force of the blast blew out the panes of glass in the front window.

All one needed was a long stick, string, and a little luck in order to enjoy a relaxing day fishing. This fishing hole was most likely somewhere along Wood River.

The building to the left is Hepworth Block. James Hepworth had a store here that sold shoes and finishing goods for gentlemen. He also ran a barbershop. Here on February 25, 1895, a checkerboard made of black walnut inlaid with white holly and cherry was exhibited. It was to be the prize given to the best checker player in Washington County at the conclusion of the annual tournament.

The cupola atop the Odd Fellows hall provided a grand view of the village and surrounding countryside. It was blown off during the Hurricane of 1938.

This photograph is a good example of Walter Rogers's ability to use natural settings to enhance the quality of his pictures.

124

Barbers Hall, also known as Chase Hall, was built in 1864 by Edward and Thomas Barber. Originally the First National Bank was on the second floor. Photographer Walter Rogers ran a tin shop and hardware store on the first floor. The bank later moved downstairs to the front of the building. The local telephone office was also located within Barbers Hall. Ed Greene, the local druggist, had a store on the first floor.

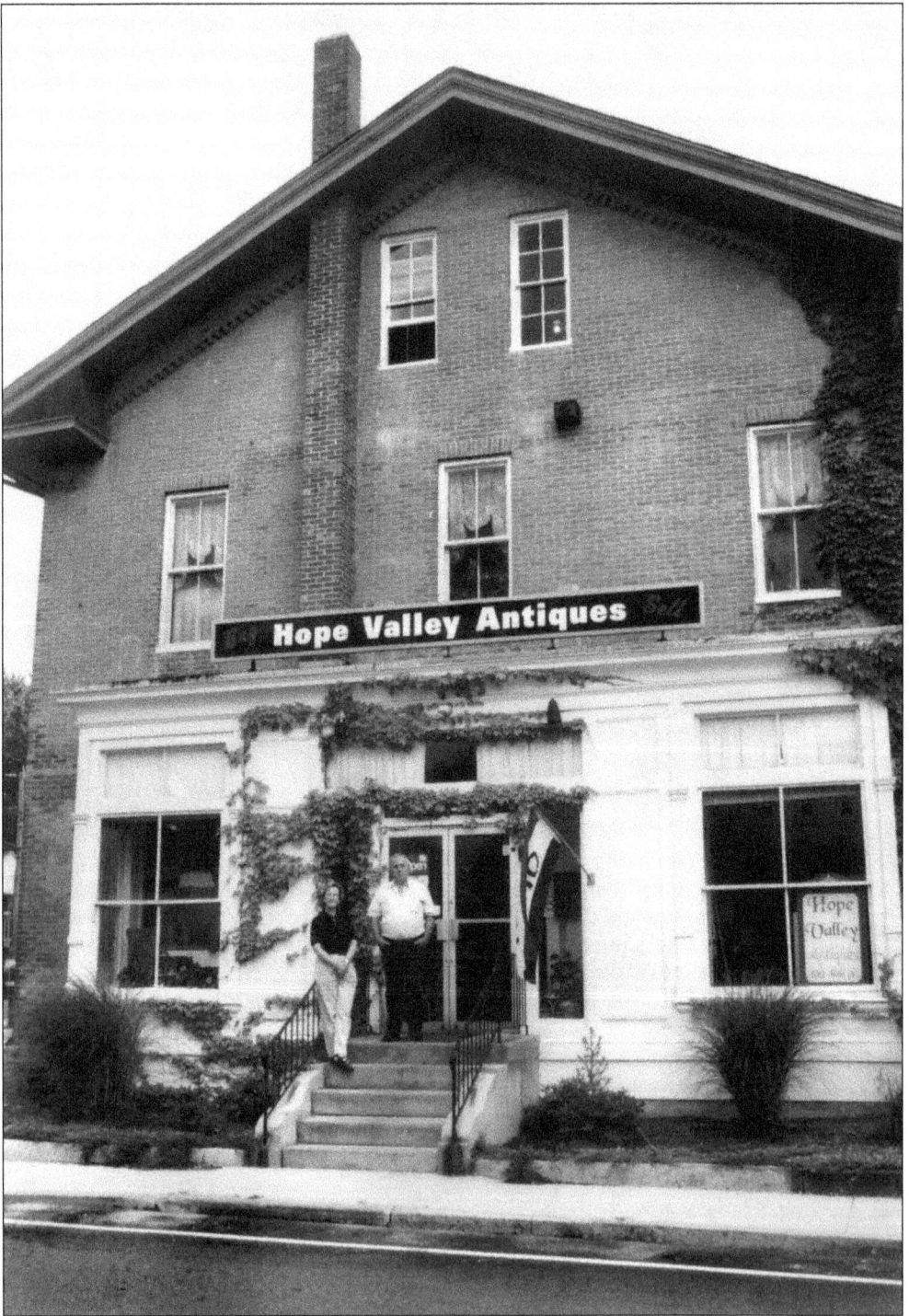

Pictured are Sandy Avery and Stephen Nichols, who operated Hope Valley Antiques. Their respect for antiquities and historical preservation is appreciated.

Hope Greene Andrews, a local historian and author, has been instrumental to this project and the identifications of many photographs taken by Walter Rogers. Hope's grandmother was Lucy Ann Nichols, the daughter of Amos Nichols. Walter Rogers married Lillian Nichols, second cousin to Amos, who was brought up in the Nichols home from childhood.

Hazel Wood (left) and Hope Greene Andrews (right) were very helpful to this project, as was the staff of the Langworthy Public Library.

I would like to thank my wife, Janice, and my daughter, Kayla, for all the support they gave me during the writing of this book.

www.ingramcontent.com/pod-product-compliance
Lightning Source LLC
Chambersburg PA
CBHW050608110426
42813CB00008B/2491